THE BOY'S *BODY* GUIDE

THE BOY'S *BODY* GUIDE

A Book For Boys 8 and Older

Frank C. Hawkins
with
Greta L.B. Laube, M.D.

Illustrated by J.C. Hawkins

www.theboysguide.com

THE BOY'S *BODY* GUIDE

The boy's body guide: a book for boys 8 and older / by Frank C. Hawkins with Greta L.B. Laube, M.D.,
illustrated by J.C. Hawkins—1st ed.

Summary: A health and hygiene guide for boys 8 and older.

Library of Congress Control Number: 2007900700
ISBN-13: 978-0-9793219-0-0
ISBN-10: 0-9793219-0-5

1. Boys—Health and hygiene—Juvenile literature.
2. Boys and puberty—Juvenile literature.

Boys Guide Books
An imprint of Big Book Press – Great Falls

FIRST EDITION

Printed in the United States of America

This book provides basic health and hygiene information. Its contents compliment, but are not a
substitute for, the direction and advice of licensed health-care professionals.

For Clay

 Boys Guide Books

Dear Friend,

One sign that you're growing up is when you start taking care of your body. But knowing *how* to do that isn't always easy. Reading this book will help. It will teach you about your body and give you some easy-to-follow tips on how to care for it.

After reading *The Boy's Body Guide*, we hope you'll talk with your parents or an adult you trust. They can answer your questions and help you find more information in the library and on the Internet. They want you to grow into a healthy and happy young man. Talk to them when you're ready.

Sincerely,

Dr. Greta and
Your Friends at
    Boys Guide Books

CONTENTS

GROWING UP

CHANGES ARE ON THE WAY!

Puberty is the name for the time when your body begins to develop and change. Not only will your body grow, but your voice will get deeper and hair will begin to sprout everywhere. Growing up to be a man means that a lot of big changes are on the way. It also means taking responsibility for the care and health of your body.

The big changes will probably start when you're 10 to 15 years old. But that's not true for everyone. You could get started earlier or even a little later. Don't worry if your best friend looks older and more grown-up. You'll catch him. Puberty starts and finishes on its own schedule—not yours.

Once puberty does begin, your body will seem to have a mind of its own. At times you'll grow so fast your shirtsleeves and pant legs will always be too short. Some boys can grow four or more inches in a year and suddenly stop. But, wait! Even after you think you're done, you could still grow a little more.

Heredity determines how tall you'll be. If your mom and dad are tall, then you'll probably be tall, too. And, if your mom and dad are not so tall, you may be the same. Nothing is for certain. To find out how tall you'll be when you're grown, you'll just have to wait and see.

HAIR

HAIR, HAIR, EVERYWHERE!

You have hair on almost every part of your body. Think about it! Some hair is easy to see, like the hair on your head. But other hair, like that on the tops of your hands and feet, is almost invisible. Depending on where it's located on your body, hair has different jobs. The hair on your head keeps your head warm. Eyelashes and eyebrows protect your eyes from dust.

One of the first signs puberty has arrived is when hair starts growing in places where it didn't before, like on your chest, under your arms, and around your genitals (also called your groin or pubic area). Your new body hair starts out thin and light-colored. Over time, it becomes thicker, curlier, and darker.

A HEAD FULL OF HAIR

Keep the hair on your head clean by washing it with a gentle shampoo and warm water. Most boys wash their hair every day, but others do it just once or twice a week. If you're an athlete or if you have oily hair, you'll probably want to wash it every day.

It's a Bugaboo!

Head lice are tiny bugs that live in your hair. Yuck! They can't jump or fly, but they have special claws that help them crawl and cling to hair. Did you know that head lice only like people's hair? Well, they do! So you don't have to worry about your dog or cat getting them.

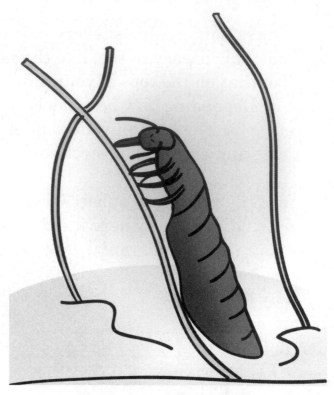

Having head lice doesn't mean you haven't washed your hair enough or that your body isn't clean. Head lice spread quickly from person to person whenever people touch their heads together or share personal items, like combs, hats, football helmets, pillows, and even sleeping bags.

Tell your mom and dad or school nurse if you feel something moving around in your hair, if your scalp itches, or if other kids you know have head lice. Your parents or the nurse can recognize head lice by looking for lice eggs (called nits). Nits are tiny yellow, tan, or brown dots attached to your hair. They look like dandruff, but you can't comb them out.

If you have head lice, don't worry! Your mom or dad can buy special medicated shampoos, creams, and lotions at the drugstore that will kill them. You'll need your parent's help applying the medicine. Be sure to carefully follow the directions to get rid of the lice and prevent them from coming back.

PEACH FUZZ

After you reach puberty, the first facial hair you notice will probably be on your chin. Some people call it "peach fuzz" because that's what it looks and feels like! Over time that peach fuzz will spread. It will get thicker, darker, and easier to see. The color and thickness of the hair on your face is hereditary. If your dad has a dark heavy beard, you'll probably have one, too. If he has a light thin beard, chances are good that's how you'll look.

Shaving is a very grown-up thing to do. When you and your parents decide it's time to start, begin with an inexpensive disposable razor and shaving cream. As you get older and your beard fills out you can try other razors and some of the many

shaving creams, gels, and foams that are available. Selecting the right razor and shaving cream depends on the thickness of your beard, the shape of your face, and the sensitivity of your skin.

IT'S SNOWING!

Does your head itch? Have you noticed light colored flakes falling from your head like snow when you scratch your head or comb your hair? It's probably dandruff, which is nothing more than dry flakes of skin from your scalp. Sometimes during puberty your oil glands don't work right, your scalp gets dry, and you develop dandruff. What you need to stop the itching and flaking is a dandruff shampoo. Ask your mom or dad to buy dandruff shampoo for you at the drugstore.

EARS

Now Hear This!

Your ears are delicate and important parts of your body. They need just a small amount of attention to stay healthy and work properly. Have your ears and hearing checked periodically. If your ears hurt or if you're having trouble hearing, talk to your parents right away and have them take you to see your family doctor.

Easy Does It

Ears are easy to clean. A wet washcloth does a really good job on the outside. And if your ears are working properly, they clean the insides by themselves. That's what the sticky yellowish wax in your ears is for. Earwax is sticky so it can trap dirt and dust before it gets too far into your ear canals. As the wax builds up it moves to the ear opening, dries up, and falls out. It doesn't get any easier than that.

If you want to clean the inside of your ears, use your index finger covered with a washcloth. Trying to clean your ear canals with a long pointed object, like a Q-Tip, will just push the wax deeper into your ear canal, making things worse. Wax is formed only in the outer part of your ear canals, not in the deep part near the eardrum. So, there is no reason to stick something deep into your ear canal to clean it.

Pop Goes Your Ears!

If you've ever flown in an airplane your ears have probably "popped." That's because the inside of your ears (the middle ear) is sensitive to air-pressure changes that happen when an airplane takes off or lands. The popping noise happens when the pressure in your middle ear is released. Usually, just swallowing or yawning will release the pressure. Chewing gum sometimes does the trick, too. If none of these methods makes your ears pop, try blowing your nose while pinching it shut.

I Can't Hear You!

Loud noise can harm your hearing. And damaged hearing usually can't be fixed. Here are some rules to follow that will protect your hearing:

- When listening to music with a headset or ear buds, keep the volume at 50% or less. If someone standing next to you can hear what you're listening to then the volume is too high.

- When you are around any loud noise, if you have to shout to be heard, then the noise is too loud. You should stop the noise or leave the area.

- When you can't avoid loud noise, wear earplugs or sound-reducing headphones.

EYES

WHAT TO LOOK FOR!

Most boys don't know they have a problem with their eyes until they have trouble reading a book or they can't see the board in school. If things look blurry or if your eyes bother you in any way,

tell your mom or dad so they can take you to see an eye doctor (optometrist or ophthalmologist). If either of your parents needed glasses when they were young, chances are you will, too.

VISION SCREENING AND EYE EXAMS

Lots of boys have their vision screened by a school nurse or family doctor. Screening is a great way to find out if you need a more thorough exam by an eye doctor. A complete eye exam takes about 30 minutes. During the exam, the doctor will check your eyes to find out how well you see. He'll also check for eye diseases that cause blindness (like glaucoma).

The eye doctor will have you read an eye chart and he'll look inside your eye using a special light and a high-powered lens. He may even use special drops to dilate (widen) the pupils of your eyes so he can check the health of your optic nerve. Or, he may give you what's called the "air-puff" test to measure the fluid pressure inside your eye. The important thing to remember about eye exams is that they're easy and they don't hurt at all.

I CAN SEE!

Getting glasses will help you see what you've been missing. Glasses are convenient and easy to wear, not to mention it's a lot easier to hit a baseball or kick a soccer ball when you can see it! Choose glasses that seem to match your personality. There are all kinds of styles—from plain to fancy. You may even have the choice to wear contact lenses. Just remember that they require special care and cleaning. Talk to your eye doctor about whether or not you should wear contact lenses, instead of glasses.

PROTECT YOUR EYES

Your eyes do great things for you, so be sure to protect them!

- Wear sunglasses with UVA/UVB protection. Too much light can give you headaches, damage your eyes, and cause vision problems when you get older (like cataracts).

- Wear eye protection when playing a sport that could injure your eyes— like hockey, racquetball, or paint ball.

- Wear safety goggles in school classes where chemicals and debris may fly through the air—such as in science, art, or shop.

MOUTH

LOOKING GOOD!

Your mouth—and everything in it—is very important to your well being. Good oral hygiene is when your mouth looks and smells healthy. This means your gums are pink, your teeth are clean and free of food, and you don't have bad breath. Good oral health makes you look and feel good, and helps you eat and speak properly.

FLOSSING

Only flossing can clean between your teeth and under your gums. A toothbrush just can't do it. Flossing removes food from between your teeth. It also scrapes plaque from the surface of your teeth and from under your gums. Plaque is a film of germs that live in your mouth and stick to your teeth. Plaque causes tooth decay and gum disease.

There are many different kinds of floss. Some is waxed and some is unwaxed. Waxed floss works better if your teeth are close together. Floss even comes in different colors and flavors! Choose one you like.

HOW TO FLOSS

- Pull out a 12-inch length of floss from the dispenser. Wrap each end around the index finger on both hands.

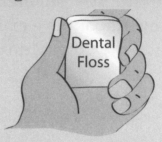

- Stretch the floss tight and use your thumbs to guide it. Push the floss between two teeth, gently moving it up and down the sides of both teeth and under the gum line.

- Floss between your other teeth the same way, taking care not to damage your gums. Don't forget to floss behind the last tooth in each row.

BRUSHING

Brush your teeth any way that works for you. Just don't scrub hard back and forth; doing that can damage your gums and tooth enamel. Most boys find that small circular motions and short back and forth motions work best. Did you know you should brush your tongue, too? It's true! Your tongue collects bacteria and dead cells that cause gum disease and bad breath. Brushing your tongue is a very good way to keep it clean.

Choose the right toothbrush. The best ones have soft, nylon, round-ended bristles. Hard bristles can injure your gums and the enamel on your teeth. And be sure that your brush is the right size for your mouth. Small-headed brushes are better since they can reach every part of your mouth, including your back teeth. Your dentist can help you choose just the right size for you. He might even suggest you use an electric toothbrush.

Replace your brush every three or four months or when the bristles start to droop. It's always a good idea to change brushes after you've had a bad cold, the flu, or strep throat, too. Thousands of germs grow on toothbrush bristles and handles. Most are harmless, but some can make you sick again, cause a gum infection, or give you a cold sore.

HOW TO BRUSH

- Hold your toothbrush at a 45-degree angle to your gum line. The bristles should contact both the tooth surface and the gum.

- Gently brush the outer tooth surfaces of two to three teeth at a time by sweeping or rolling the brush away from the gum line. Do the same for the inner tooth surfaces.

- Tilt your toothbrush vertically behind your front teeth. Make several up and down strokes on the backs of the upper and lower front teeth.

- Clean the biting surfaces of your teeth by using a gentle back and forth scrubbing motion.

- Gently brush your tongue from back to front to remove bacteria.

It's also important that you use the right toothpaste. Select toothpaste that contains fluoride. Fluoride protects your teeth from decay. Ask your dentist which toothpaste is right for you if you're not sure. And remember, you need only a squirt about the size of a pea to do the job right.

TIME TO FLOSS AND BRUSH AGAIN?

It's best to brush your teeth after breakfast and at bedtime. You should floss your teeth at least once a day to remove food and plaque. Plaque is that film of bacteria that leads to cavities and gum infections. If you can only floss and brush once a day, do it before bedtime. Plaque and food do the most damage at night while you sleep. After flossing, try to spend at least two minutes brushing. Remember: floss, then brush.

OFF TO SEE THE DENTIST!

See your dentist regularly. It's a must. One visit every six months is usually enough to keep your teeth clean and your gums healthy.

I Have Braces, What Now?

Braces straighten your teeth. They will improve your appearance and your health. You probably already know someone who has them. That's not surprising because lots of people—not only boys, but also grown men and even sports stars—wear braces.

Some braces are made from very fine metal wire; others are clear or the same color as your teeth. There are even braces that fit behind your teeth so no one will know you're wearing them. Unless you tell them, of course!

Braces trap food, so you need to work extra hard to keep your teeth clean while you have them. Brushing your teeth carefully and regularly—like after every meal and snack—is a good idea. Take extra care to clean hard-to-reach places around brackets and under wires. And be sure to ask your dentist or orthodontist for a special brush that will make the job easier.

While you have braces, you'll want to avoid foods that can break them or get stuck in them. Try not to eat popcorn, hard candies like lemon drops, sticky candies like caramels, and especially gum. Sugary sodas and juices are bad, too, because the sugar stays on your teeth and can cause tooth decay behind the brackets and wires if you don't brush afterward.

COLD SORES—OUCH!

Cold sores (also called fever blisters) are small, painful, fluid-filled blisters that show up one at a time or in little bunches. They usually occur on your lips and they last 7 to 10 days. Just to let you know, you don't need to have a cold to get a cold sore. And you don't need a fever to have a fever blister!

Cold sores are very common and very contagious. Once you catch the virus that causes them, it stays in your body waiting around for another time to come out and cause more sores. Cold sores usually come back in the same place as previous ones.

Cold sores generally clear up without treatment in a week or so. But you may want to speed up the healing process by trying some of the cold-sore medicines at the drugstore. There are many different products that dry up and heal cold sores. Some work better than others, so try them until you find the one that works best for you. If you get a lot of cold sores, your parents may take you to see your family doctor. He or she can give you a special cream that will speed the healing even faster and reduce the pain.

While you're waiting for the cold sore to go away, remember to wash your hands regularly and don't pick at it. You don't want to spread the virus to other parts of your body, like your eyes or groin.

20

HANDS

BUSY HANDS

Your hands cover your mouth when you sneeze, help you go to the bathroom, and empty your cat's litter box. There's not much your hands don't touch, and they can get very dirty.

Dirty hands can make you sick. Touching other people or dirty surfaces, like toilet seats and bathroom doorknobs, can pass the germs that cause colds, flu, diarrhea, and stomach aches from person to person. Once the germs are on your hands, all you have to do is rub your eyes or nose to expose yourself to them and get sick.

CLEAN HANDS

Stay healthy by washing your hands after sneezing or coughing, before eating or preparing food, after using the bathroom, after cleaning up after your pet, and anytime your hands are dirty. And be sure to wash your hands more often than usual if someone around you is sick. Washing your hands is a very good habit.

WHISTLE WHILE YOU WASH

- Wet your hands with warm water and then lather up with soap. Soap kills germs.

- Rub your hands together and scrub all the surfaces, including your palms, wrists, between your fingers, and under your nails.

- Rub and scrub for about as long as it takes to whistle one verse of "Row, Row, Row Your Boat".

- Rinse and dry your hands on a paper towel or clean cloth.

- In public bathrooms, turn off the water using the towel to avoid getting germs on your clean hands. You can use the same towel to open the door. Door handles are great carriers of germs.

- When you can't wash your hands with soap and water, a good alternative is to use a hand-sanitizing wipe or gel.

FINGERNAILS

Your fingernails protect the tips of your fingers. They make it easier to scratch an itch and pick up a penny. Fingernails are made from the same protein as your hair and the top layer of your skin.

Trim your fingernails once a week with special scissors or clippers made just for the job. Trim them straight across, slightly rounding the nail at the top. If you get a hangnail—a little tag of skin around your fingernail that hurts—clip it as short as you can and leave it alone. Biting or picking at a hangnail only makes it worse, and could cause an infection.

WARTS

Warts are skin infections caused by viruses passed from one person to another. And, no, you can't get a wart from holding a frog or toad! Warts are a small hard bump that's often grayish-brown in color. They usually have a rough surface that looks like the head of a cauliflower with black dots inside. If you pick at a wart, it can spread to other parts of your body.

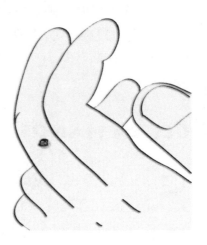

Most warts go away by themselves in two to three years. Your parents can buy you wart-removal medications at the drugstore if you can't wait that long. Some boys treat their warts by covering them with a piece of duct tape. Try it if you want to. Your family doctor also has several ways (burning, freezing, or prescription medication) to remove the wart and keep it from spreading further.

FEET

OH, MY ACHING FEET!

Your feet take a real pounding every time you take a step. But you probably don't pay much attention to them unless they itch or hurt. With just a little preventive care, though, your feet will help you stand up to be counted, walk all over town with your friends, and run the 100-yard dash.

ATHLETE'S FOOT

Athletes aren't the only people who get athlete's foot. It's a common skin infection caused by a fungus that eats old skin cells. The fungus grows on warm damp surfaces around swimming pools, school locker rooms, and public showers. When you walk barefoot in these places the fungus ends up on your feet.

If you have itchy, cracked, blistered, or peeling areas between your toes, or on the bottoms of your feet, you probably have athlete's foot. Don't scratch and don't worry! Athlete's foot is easy to treat with any of the sprays, powders, or creams available at the drugstore.

TOENAILS

Your toenails grow a lot slower than your fingernails so you don't have to trim them as often. But when you do, it's a tough job. The best time is after a shower or bath when they're soft. Use the same scissors or clippers you use for your fingernails. Trim them straight across to avoid an ingrown toenail. That's when a sharp corner of your toenail grows into the skin. Ouch!

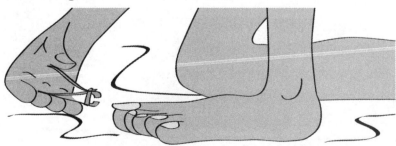

STINKY FEET!

Your feet work so hard that sometimes they get sweaty and stinky. The bacteria that live on your feet are what make them smell. These bacteria love dark damp places, like the inside of sweaty shoes. And if you don't wear socks, they love it even more. The best remedies for stinky feet are to wash your feet, wear clean socks, and air out your shoes. Sprinkle baking soda in your shoes or use an anti-bacterial spray from the drugstore to make them smell better.

PLANTAR WARTS

"Plantar wart" is a fancy name for a wart on the bottom of your foot. A plantar wart makes you feel like you have a stone in your shoe all the time. It really hurts when you walk!

Just like warts on your hands, plantar warts are skin infections caused by viruses passed from one person to another. A very common place to catch a plantar wart is in a public shower or school locker room. When you're in one of these places, wear sandals or flip-flops instead of going barefoot.

It's a good idea to remove a plantar wart as soon as possible. They're more difficult to get rid of than a wart on your hand, though. A popular way for boys to treat a plantar wart is to use duct tape on it. If that doesn't work fast enough for you, have your parents take you to see your family doctor or a foot doctor (podiatrist). They'll have several ways to help you get rid of that plantar wart, including prescription medications and laser treatments.

CHECK OUT THOSE SHOES!

When you buy shoes, make sure they fit right. Toes should have a 1/2-inch clearance, but not much more. (That's about one size larger than your foot measures). And did you know that both of your feet might not be exactly the same length or width? It's true! So before you say "yes" when buying new shoes, walk around the store in them. Make sure they feel good on your feet and the heels don't slip. A different size or width can make a big difference. Even if they really rock, don't get shoes if they don't fit right.

SKIN

SKIN IS AN ORGAN

Your skin is an organ, just like your heart, liver, and lungs. In fact, it's the biggest organ in your body! Your skin is covered with tiny holes called pores. The pores contain oil glands that moisten your skin and hair.

Your skin is a container that holds your insides—a wrapper that protects you from infections and keeps you from getting sick. Your skin warms you when you're cold and cools you when you're hot. Sounds important, huh? That's why it's a good idea to take care of your skin.

What Do Whiteheads, Blackheads, Pimples, and Cysts Have in Common?

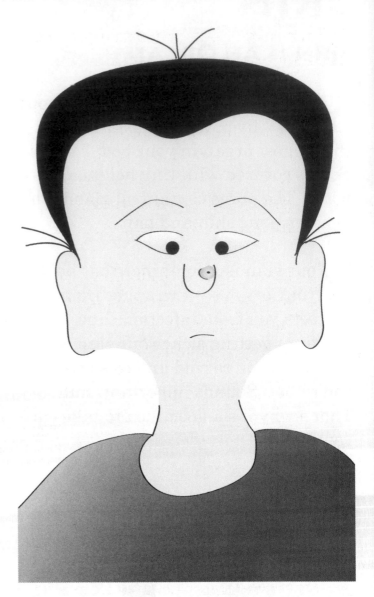

Answer? They are all types of acne! Your skin's pores sometimes get clogged up with oil, dead skin cells, and germs (bacteria). When a pore clogs up, closes, and bulges out from the skin, it's called a *whitehead*. When a pore clogs up but stays open, the top surface usually gets dark and presto you have a *blackhead*. At other times, the walls of the pore break, allowing oil, dead skin cells, and bacteria to get under your skin. This causes a small red infected bump called a *pimple*. When a pore clogs up and the infection goes deeper and fills with puss, it's called a *cyst*.

Wow, that's a lot to remember! But don't worry about it. Just remember that if either of your parents had acne, chances are very good that you will, too. Don't feel alone. Almost everyone has acne of some kind by the time they become an adult. The good news is that most acne goes away about the time you turn 20 years old. Still, it's not easy to look at yourself in the mirror and see a big fat pimple on your nose.

There are things you can do to keep acne breakouts to a minimum.

1. Wash your face twice a day with soap and warm water.

2. Don't scrub your face. Wash gently, using your fingertips instead of a washcloth.

3. If you wear sunscreen on your face, make sure it's labeled "nonacnegenic" or "noncomedogenic."

4. Wash your face after you've been exercising and sweating a lot.

5. Don't touch, squeeze, or pop pimples. The oil and dirt from your hands will just make things worse.

6. Try some of the acne lotions and creams from your drugstore to see if they help. The ones that contain benzyl peroxide (kills bacteria) are usually the best.

7. If your acne is more serious, a family doctor or dermatologist (skin doctor) can prescribe stronger creams and lotions.

DID YOU KNOW?

- Stress doesn't cause acne.

- Eating fried foods and chocolate doesn't cause acne.

- Getting a tan on your face doesn't make acne better. Too much sun can, however, dry out your skin and give you painful sunburn with more serious consequences than having acne.

- Washing and scrubbing your face a gazillion times a day does not make acne go away. It only dries out your skin and makes the acne worse. Washing two times a day is enough.

WHAT ARE THOSE SPOTS ON YOUR FACE?

If you have freckles it doesn't mean you have a problem with your skin or there's anything wrong with your health. Freckles are just skin cells that contain color (pigment). The sun causes the pigment (known as melanin) to brown (tan) unevenly resulting in freckles. Freckles are usually light brown, flat, and smaller than the head of a pin. Sometimes they look bigger because they overlap and run together.

You can't get rid of your freckles, but wearing sunscreen and a hat will cut down on how many you have. For some boys, freckles fade in the winter and return with the sun in the summer. For other boys, freckles don't change much with or without the sun. As you get older, your freckles will probably fade more each year.

Make the most of your freckles! They give you a distinct look—something that makes you unique. Wear your freckles proudly!

SUN SAFETY

Ultraviolet rays (called UV rays for short) from the sun will burn your skin. You can get sunburned on sunny *and* cloudy days. And if you get burned too many times, it can lead to allergic reactions, wrinkled skin, and skin cancer when you get older. Sun damage to your skin takes time and it probably seems like it can't happen to you. It can! Be careful!

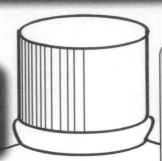

All boys sunburn, but boys with light-colored skin sunburn more quickly.

Apply sunscreen to exposed skin. Don't forget the back of your neck, the tops of your feet, your face, the backs of your legs, and your ears.

If you're swimming or boating, you'll get sunburned faster because the sun's rays reflect off the sand and water.

SUN SCREEN

SPF 45

Protect Your Skin

The sun's rays are strongest between 10:00 in the morning and 4:00 in afternoon.

Always use a sunscreen with a sun protection factor (SPF) rating of 45 or higher. It's a good idea to put on the sunscreen again every 2-3 hours, especially if you're swimming or sweating a lot.

Take regular breaks from the sun by going indoors or moving into the shade.

Clothing, like hats, shirts, and pants, protect you from the sun. Just make sure the clothing is made from a material the sun's rays won't pass through.

DO THESE THINGS TO HEAL YOUR SKIN AND FEEL BETTER IF YOU GET SUNBURNED:

Moisturize your sunburned skin with an Aloe Vera-based cream, lotion, or spray. Don't use petroleum-based products, like Vaseline, because they trap heat and sweat.

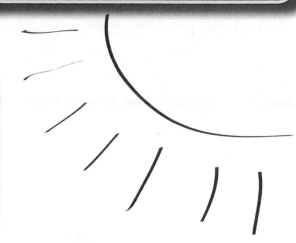

Take a cool bath or shower.

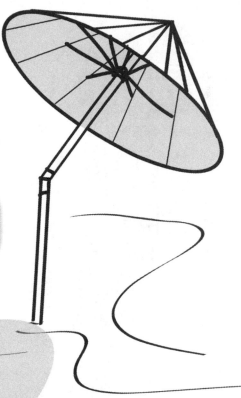

Stay out of the sun until your skin heals.

Tell your parents if you have blisters from the sun. Don't scratch or pop them because they can get infected and leave scars.

BLISTERS

A blister is a raised area of skin with watery fluid inside. Blisters are caused by friction, like when your foot rubs against a shoe that doesn't fit right. Blisters usually heal by themselves. Just keep them clean and dry and cover them with a band-aid until they go away. While the blister's healing, be careful not to irritate the area further. Otherwise, it won't heal.

SWEAT IS COOL!

Did you know your skin has a special cooling system? Well, it does! Your skin is covered with glands that make sweat (also called perspiration). When your body gets hot, those glands start working. The sweat they make comes out through the pores in your skin and makes your skin wet. The evaporation of the sweat from your skin is what cools you down. But it takes lots of fluid to make sweat. That's why it's important to put fluids back into your body by drinking plenty of water so you won't get dehydrated.

THAT SMELL CAN'T BE ME!

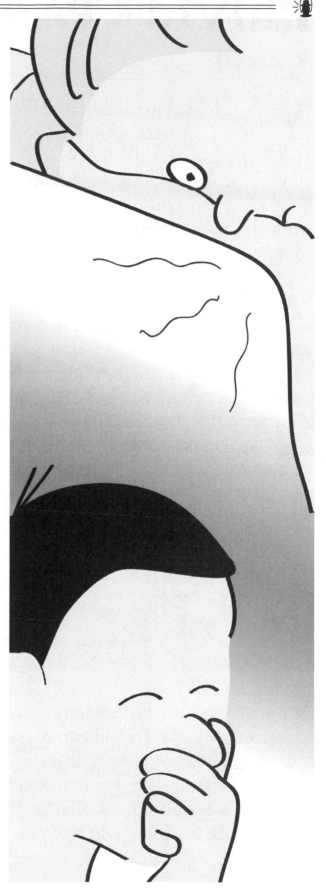

Oh, yes it can! As you go through puberty, there are special sweat glands that start working for the first time. These glands are found only under your arms and around your genitals. The sweat from them contains proteins and carbohydrates that mix with the bacteria on your skin to cause an awful smell. Showering with warm water and cleaning with a mild soap will wash away the bacteria and help control your body odor. Wearing clean clothes, socks, and underwear every day will also help.

If you (and maybe other people around you) don't like the way your underarms smell, you can use a deodorant or antiperspirant. The difference between deodorants and antiperspirants is that deodorants cover up the smell while antiperspirants stop or dry up the sweat. They are two different ways to solve the same problem. Try both and see which you like best.

PRIVATE PARTS

YOUCH!

Your private parts consist of your penis and the sac that hangs below your penis called the scrotum. The scrotum contains two small organs called testicles. Nothing hurts worse than getting hit in your privates. Why? It's because your privates aren't protected by bones and muscles like your other organs—your heart, lungs, and kidneys. Your privates are easily injured because they're exposed and because they're very sensitive.

As you may have already learned the hard way, there are lots of ways to hurt your privates. You can get hurt playing baseball, skateboarding, or just horsing around with your friends. As you get older, it's probably a good idea to wear an athletic supporter (also called a jock or jockstrap) when you play sports. If you play a contact sport, like football or soccer, you should make sure your jock also has a cup to protect you from bruising or rupture.

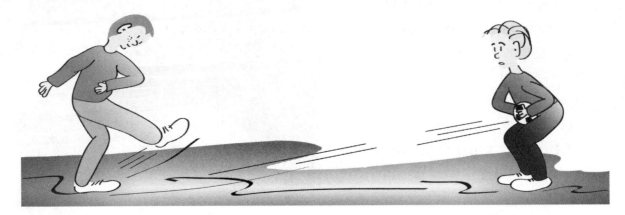

Injuries to your privates are usually not serious, though they cause a lot of pain and can make you feel sick to your stomach for as long as one hour. Applying ice and taking pain relievers can help reduce the pain. If the pain doesn't go away in an hour, if your scrotum is bruised or swollen, or if you develop a fever, you should tell your dad or mom and have them take you to see your family doctor.

How Things Change!

Doctors divide development of your private parts into five stages. The changes start when puberty starts and they end when puberty ends. What stage are you?

Stage 1: Before puberty begins, you don't have any pubic hair, and your penis and testicles haven't begun to change.

Stage 2: Pubic hair begins to grow. It is sparse, long, and lightly colored. Your testicles also begin to get larger. Your penis may grow slightly or not at all at this stage.

Stage 3: Your pubic hair begins to spread. It gets darker, coarser, and curlier. Your testicles continue to get larger and your penis gets longer.

Stage 4: Pubic hair covers the base of your penis and begins to grow on the upper part of your scrotum. The hair gets even darker, coarser, and curlier. Your testicles continue to grow, and your penis gets longer and wider.

Stage 5: Your pubic hair has spread to the inside of your thighs, and your testicles and penis have grown to their final adult size and shape.

Stage 1 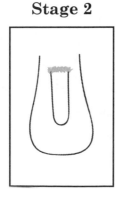 Stage 2  Stage 3 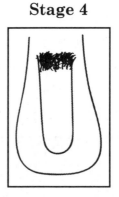 Stage 4 Stage 5

ATTEN-HUT!

When your penis fills with blood it gets hard and stands out from your body. This is called an "erection." As you reach puberty, you'll notice that you're having more and more erections. They can happen at any time of the day or night, even when you're sleeping.

If you ever wake up and find your pajamas wet, chances are you had what's called a "wet dream." That's when fluid from your testicles—called "semen"— comes out of your penis while you're asleep. Almost every boy has had wet dreams from time to time. It's a sign you're growing up.

STOP! YOU'LL GO BLIND!

As you reach the end of puberty, you'll become more interested in sex and start thinking about it. Masturbation is when you rub your penis because you like the way it feels. Sometimes the rubbing gives you an "orgasm" and semen comes out of your penis.

People say all sorts of things about masturbation. You might hear them say it causes disease, stunts your growth, and leads to blindness. Some may even say it causes you to grow hair on the palms of your hands! Don't believe it. Not one word is true!

There is one thing for sure, though. Most people consider masturbation to be personal. They don't like talking about it because it makes them feel uncomfortable. For that reason, a lot of funny and not-so-funny stories get started and that's when you might hear things that aren't true. If you have questions about masturbation, talk to a trusted family member or your family doctor.

MEASURING UP

Just about every boy wonders how his penis measures up. Is it too small? Is it shaped right? Well, here's the truth about penises: They come in all shapes and sizes. How your penis looks is hereditary, like the color of your eyes, the size of your feet, and the shape of your nose. And despite what you hear and read, you can't change how your penis looks or how big it is.

There's no good or bad when it comes to penis size. Some of it depends on how old you are. You wouldn't expect someone who's 10 years old to look the same as someone who's 20. And, just for the record, there's a lot less difference in penis size between boys of the same age when they get an erection than when their penises are soft.

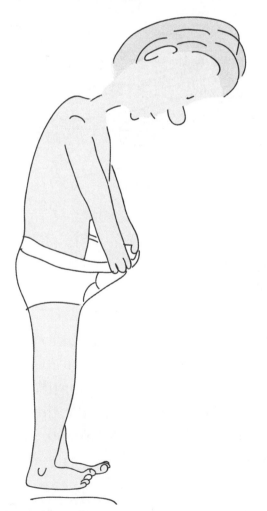

Every boy's penis looks a little different. And just like size, there's no good or bad when it comes to how your penis looks and is shaped. Some hang to the left and others hang to the right. Either way is OK. Some are circumcised and others are not. Either way is OK. Circumcision is when the skin that covers the tip of the penis is removed to expose the head (also called the glans). Your parents decided after you were born whether or not you should be circumcised.

One last bit of advice: Don't spend too much time comparing yourself to other boys. You're in a class by yourself. And that's OK.

EATING RIGHT

"I'll Have The French Fries, Please!"

French fries are potatoes. And potatoes are good for you, right? But wait a minute! Did you know french fries aren't really good for you? It's true! French fries are fried in oil. As they cook they soak up the oil, which is really just fat. And all that fat can make you fat—especially if you eat fried foods like french fries every day.

The U.S. National Heart, Lung, and Blood Institute (www.nhlbi.nih.gov) has a chart they call "*GO, SLOW and WHOA Foods.*" *GO* foods and drinks are the lowest in fat, sugar and calories. They are rich in vitamins, minerals and other nutrients important to your health. They help you grow strong and healthy. *SLOW* foods and drinks are higher in fat, added sugar, and calories than *GO* foods. They're not as good for you. *WHOA* foods and drinks are the highest in fat, added sugar, and calories. They'll ruin your health if you eat them too often.

40

Go, Slow, and Whoa Foods (and Drinks)

GO: Eat almost anytime.

SLOW: Eat sometimes, at most several times a week.

WHOA: Eat only once in a while or for special treats.

	GO	SLOW	WHOA
Vegetables	Almost all fresh, frozen, and canned vegetables without added fat and sauces	All vegetables with added fat and sauces; oven-baked french fries; avocado	Fried potatoes, like french fries and hash browns; vegetables fried in oil
Fruits	Fresh and frozen fruits; fruits canned in their juice	100% fruit juice; fruits canned in light syrup; dried fruits	Fruits canned in heavy syrup
Breads and Cereals	Whole-grain breads; pita bread; tortillas; pasta; brown rice; whole-grain cereals with no added sugar	White refined flour bread, rice, and pasta; french toast; taco shells; corn bread; biscuits; waffles; pancakes; biscuits; granola	Croissants; muffins; doughnuts; sweet rolls; cereals with added sugar
Milk and Milk Products	Fat-free or 1% milk; fat-free or low-fat yogurt; part skim, reduced fat, and fat-free cheese; low-fat or fat-free cottage cheese	2% low-fat milk; processed cheese spread	Whole milk; cheese (like American, cheddar, and Swiss); cream cheese; yogurt made with whole milk
Meats, Chicken, Fish, Eggs, Beans, and Nuts	Trimmed beef and pork; extra lean ground beef; chicken and turkey without skin; tuna canned in water; baked, broiled, steamed, and grilled fish; beans; split peas; lentils	Lean ground beef; broiled hamburgers; ham; chicken and turkey with skin; tuna canned in oil; peanut butter; nuts	Untrimmed beef and pork; regular ground beef; fried hamburgers; ribs; bacon; fried chicken, chicken nuggets; hot dogs; lunch meats; pepperoni, sausage; fried fish
Sweets and Snacks	Frozen fruit juice bars; low-fat frozen yogurt and ice-cream; fig bars; baked chips; low-fat popcorn; pretzels		Cookies; cakes; pies; ice cream; chocolate; candy; chips; buttered popcorn
Fats (Stuff that goes on or in your food)	Ketchup; mustard; fat-free salad dressing; fat-free mayonnaise; fat-free sour cream; vegetable oil; olive oil; oil-based salad dressing	Low-fat salad dressing; low-fat mayonnaise; low-fat sour cream	Butter; margarine; gravy; regular creamy salad dressing; mayonnaise; tartar sauce; sour cream; cheese sauce; cream sauce
Drinks	Water; diet soda; diet lemonade	100% fruit juice; sports drinks	Regular soda; sweetened iced tea; lemonade; fruit drinks with less than 100% fruit juice

41

VITAMINS AND MINERALS

What makes a young man strong and healthy? A balanced diet with all the right vitamins and minerals! Here are the main vitamins and minerals you need and the foods you can eat to get them.

THE B VITAMINS

Give you energy, muscle tone, and healthy hair, skin, and eyes. Eat meat, fish, chicken, whole wheat breads, leafy green vegetables, dried beans, peas, and soybeans.

VITAMIN C

Helps fight infection and heal cuts. It also helps you have healthy skin, bones, teeth and blood vessels. Eat oranges (or drink orange juice), strawberries, tomatoes, broccoli, turnip greens and other greens, sweet and white potatoes, and cantaloupe.

ZINC

Helps your body fight illness and infection. Eat beef, pork, beans, peas, and peanuts.

One-a-Day
MultiVitamin
MultiMineral

Nature's Finest

VITAMIN E

Keeps your skin, heart, nerves, muscles, and red blood cells healthy. Eat wheat germ, corn, nuts, seeds, olives, spinach, asparagus, and other leafy vegetables.

VITAMIN A

Helps prevent and fight infections. It also helps you see and your bones grow. Eat carrots, pumpkin, sweet potatoes, cantaloupe, red grapefruit, apricots, broccoli, and spinach.

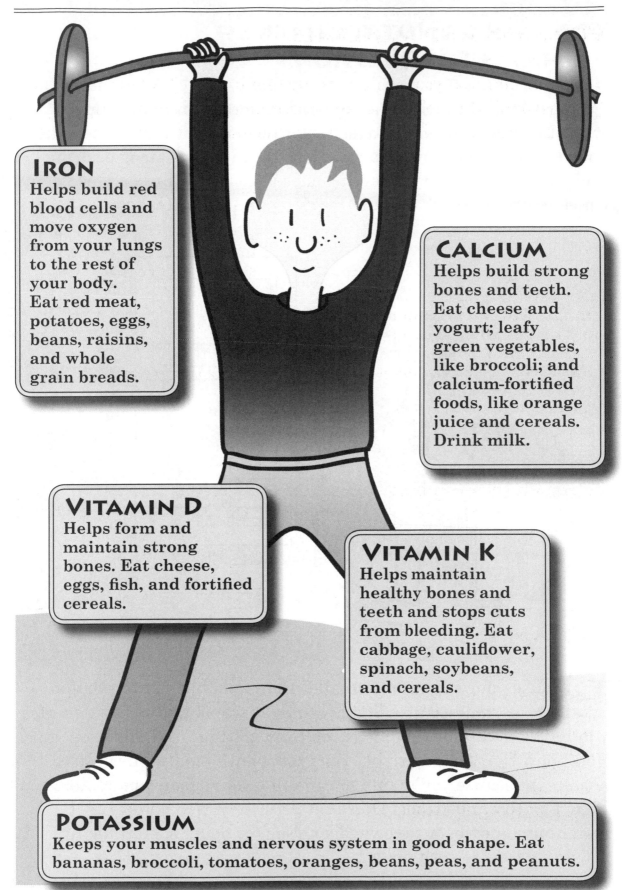

IRON
Helps build red blood cells and move oxygen from your lungs to the rest of your body. Eat red meat, potatoes, eggs, beans, raisins, and whole grain breads.

CALCIUM
Helps build strong bones and teeth. Eat cheese and yogurt; leafy green vegetables, like broccoli; and calcium-fortified foods, like orange juice and cereals. Drink milk.

VITAMIN D
Helps form and maintain strong bones. Eat cheese, eggs, fish, and fortified cereals.

VITAMIN K
Helps maintain healthy bones and teeth and stops cuts from bleeding. Eat cabbage, cauliflower, spinach, soybeans, and cereals.

POTASSIUM
Keeps your muscles and nervous system in good shape. Eat bananas, broccoli, tomatoes, oranges, beans, peas, and peanuts.

To Snack or Not to Snack
— That Is The Question!

Here's the situation: It's two hours before dinner and you're starving. Your mom says, "No snacks. I don't want you to ruin your dinner!" The truth is a snack is OK if it's a GO food or drink and you're still hungry when it comes time to eat dinner. Good times to grab a snack are mid-morning and mid-afternoon.

Because your stomach is smaller than an adult's stomach and because you use up a lot of energy at school and playing sports, you have to eat more often to keep from getting tired and grouchy. You know that feeling, right? But, you want to make sure you're snacking because you're hungry and in need of good food to help you grow healthy and strong. Don't eat because you're bored, or watching a movie, or to reward yourself for doing something like finishing a homework project.

et's say it's 10 o'clock in the morning, you just finished gym class, and you're getting hungry. What should you eat? Some good choices would be an apple, orange, yogurt, popcorn, peanut butter crackers, cheese, or a piece of whole-grain bread. Eat something you like, but try your best to avoid treats like candy bars, chips, and sodas that fill you up fast and will make you feel tired even faster. Remember: "Snack" doesn't mean junk food!

INSTEAD OF ...	HOW ABOUT ...
Ice cream	Fruit smoothies
Milk shakes	Fruit
Hard candy	Frozen yogurt
Regular potato chips	Baked Pretzels
Cookies	Water
Cinnamon buns	Baked potato chips
Soda	Butter-free popcorn
Fruit juice	Whole-grain bagel
Buttered popcorn	Fig bars
Candy bars	Water or Low-fat milk

EXERCISE AND FITNESS

THE BASICS

Exercise and fitness are two peas in a pod. Every time you exercise you're taking another step on your way to being fit. Playing kickball at school is a kind of exercise. So is playing soccer, doing sit-ups, and even reaching down to touch your toes. Spend less time watching TV and playing video games. Exercise makes your body strong and healthy. Find a sport or game you like and do it regularly.

I WANT MUSCLES— NOW!

So, when do you get muscles? The truth is it's hard to say. Just like hair and everything else that happens during puberty, muscles happen when your body says it's time. You might be considering lifting weights to make your muscles bigger. Wait until you reach puberty to start. Lifting weights before then won't build bigger muscles and it could injure you. In the meantime, eat healthy foods and stay active playing sports and riding your bike. That will keep you strong, fit, and ready to start building muscles when your body's ready.

When it's time, here are some things to consider:

1. Find someone who's experienced to help you learn how to lift weights, like a coach or trainer. There's a right and a wrong way. Lifting the right way will help you gain strength and develop muscles. Lifting the wrong way can injure your body.

2. Do two or three sets of 10 to 15 repetitions using lighter weights instead of one set of 1 to 5 repetitions using heavy weights to "bulk" up. Lighter weights and more repetitions build muscle safely. Heavy weights can injure you and delay your progress.

3. Don't work the same muscle group (chest, back, arms, and legs) two days in a row. Your muscles need at least a day's rest before you work them again.

You may also have heard that taking steroids will make your muscles bigger and make you a better athlete. What you don't hear is that anabolic steroids—the kind some athletes take to help them cheat—are illegal because they are very dangerous and bad for your health.

Anabolic steroids have lots of immediate side effects, including acne, oily hair, swelling of your legs and feet, and they can stunt your growth. The long-term effects are even worse, including hair loss, hallucinations (seeing things that aren't there), high blood pressure, heart disease, liver damage, and pain when you pee.

Some food supplements contain anabolic steroids. You can see advertisements for them on the Internet or in most bodybuilding magazines. Some of the supplements are legal and others are illegal. But legal or illegal, these supplements can cause health problems for a young growing body like yours. Don't take any steroid supplements, even those that look legal and are advertised in your favorite bodybuilding magazine.

PLAY SAFE!

Playing sports is fun; getting hurt is not. Here are the six basic rules of sports safety:

1. Warm Up and S-T-R-E-T-C-H Out

Before exercising—whether it's a pick-up game of baseball or the soccer finals—take a few minutes to prepare your body for the work out that's coming. Warm up by jogging or doing jumping jacks to increase your blood flow and muscle temperature. Finish getting ready by doing some slow, gradual stretching to lengthen your muscles to prevent muscle pulls and tears. Take some time after your game to stretch a little so your muscles won't tighten up and hurt later on. Talk to your coach to get some pointers on the right way to stretch before and after exercising.

2. Use the Right Equipment

Make sure you wear the right protective gear for the sport you're playing. Almost every sport has specially designed gear to protect you. Talk with your parents or your coach to know what gear you need. Different style helmets are worn in baseball, biking, skateboarding, football, hockey, and skating. Wearing cleats helps your feet grip the ground and avoid ankle and leg injuries when playing football, baseball, softball, and soccer. Other sports require pads (such as wrist, elbow, and knee guards); eye protection; mouth guards; or a jockstrap. And don't forget to wear the gear correctly: If you don't fasten the strap on your helmet, it will fall off when you need it most. It doesn't matter whether you're practicing or playing the big game. Wear your protective gear!

3. Follow the Rules

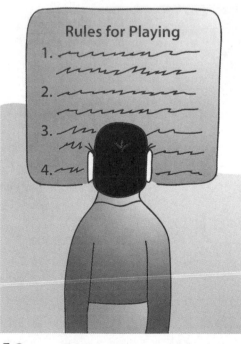

Every game has its own set of rules. That's so everybody playing knows what to expect. In football, it's OK to tackle the guy with the ball. But what if someone tackled you in basketball? Not only is it against the rules, there's a pretty good chance you'd be hurt. When everyone knows the rules of the game—what's legal and what's not— fewer people are hurt. Games are always more fun—and safer—when you know and play by the rules.

4. Don't Play If You're Injured

Sure it's important not to let your teammates and coach down, but if you're hurt, no one expects you to keep on playing. Playing after you've been hurt will probably make the injury even worse and put you on the sideline for a long time. The same goes for playing again before an injury has the chance to heal completely. Be honest with your parents and coach if you've been hurt and follow his or her advice about when to play again.

5. Drink Plenty of Water

Sweating makes the water level in your body go down. And when you're playing sports, it happens really fast. Just like a car radiator, you want to keep the water level from dropping too low. Don't wait until you're thirsty to begin drinking water. Take a bottle of water with you to soccer practice or to play in the park. And drink up!

6. Don't Over Heat

What's hotter than an afternoon football scrimmage in August? Not much! It's easy to get heat exhaustion when you're exercising in the sun or on a hot day. Remember how sweat cools your skin as it evaporates? Well, heat exhaustion happens when your body can't cool itself fast enough. It comes on quickly and makes you feel overheated, tired, and weak. Sometimes when people get heat exhaustion, they collapse on the ground right in the middle of a game. It can make you feel tired for days after it happens.

Heat stroke is even more serious. Be on the look out for heat stroke if you stop sweating, get a high temperature, and your skin is red-colored and hot to the touch. Also, people who are having a heat stroke will probably be uncoordinated, confused, or even lose consciousness. Tell an adult right away if you have a headache, get dizzy, or feel like you're going to throw up. You'll want to get out of the sun and drink liquids. Heat stroke requires immediate medical attention.

SLEEP

EVERYBODY'S DOING IT!

Everyone sleeps. It's how your body recharges itself so you'll be ready to get up tomorrow feeling rested, healthy, and strong. Most boys between the ages of 8 and 12 need about 10 hours of sleep every night. But between after-school activities, homework, and everything else going on, it's hard to find time to get the sleep your body needs. Try hard, though, it's important that you get enough rest so you can be your best at school, sports, and in life.

TIPS TO SLEEP BY

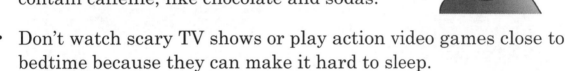

- Play hard and eat right during the day.

- After dinner, limit foods and drinks that contain caffeine, like chocolate and sodas.

- Don't watch scary TV shows or play action video games close to bedtime because they can make it hard to sleep.

- Organize yourself and take the pressure off the next morning by packing your lunch, laying out your clothes, collecting your homework, and getting your backpack ready.

- Go to bed around the same time every night; this helps your body get on a schedule.

- Floss, brush, and take a warm shower every night; this tells your body it's time for bed.

- Tune out the noise when it's time to fall asleep. Turn off your MP3 player, computer, and TV.

- Get comfortable in bed.

- Relax. Think about things that make you happy.

STILL CAN'T SLEEP?

There's usually a good reason you can't fall asleep. It could be a test at school you're worried about, or something someone said that hurt or angered you. As you lie in bed you may keep thinking about it over and over in your head. And guess what happens? You can't fall asleep. Think the problem through and talk to someone about it, like your mom or dad or a friend. Don't be embarrassed because you have feelings. That's a good thing! Even if the problem can't be solved, just talking it out will help you relax and get some sleep.

It's also possible you're too hot, too cold, too hungry, or too crowded in bed to fall asleep. Turn on a fan if you're hot. Put socks on if you're cold. Eat a light snack if you're hungry. And, make sure your bed isn't jammed with so much stuff there's no room for you. If none of that works, try this technique to fall asleep: First, start with your toes and concentrate on completely relaxing them. When your toes are relaxed, do the same for your feet. Then, one at a time, do your ankles, legs, hands, and arms. Before you know it, you'll be sound asleep.

WHEN DREAMS GET SCARY

Have you ever been so scared you couldn't scream? Nightmares can do that to you. Everybody dreams. And everybody has nightmares once in a while. The good thing about nightmares is that no matter how real they seem, they're only dreams. They aren't real and they can't hurt you.

Stressful things that happen during the day can turn good dreams into bad dreams. Nightmares are almost always connected to something that happened to you or something you saw during the day. Watching a violent movie or reading a scary book can give you nightmares. Problems at school, stress from homework, or problems at home can give you nightmares, too.

If you're having nightmares, try these ideas to get them under control:

1. Talk to your mom or dad or a friend about the nightmare and how it makes you feel.

2. Sleep with something that makes you feel more secure.

3. Open your bedroom door so you can hear and talk to your family.

4. Use a nightlight so that if you wake up suddenly, you can see where you are.

5. Write your dreams—good and bad—in a journal exactly as you remember them. A list of dreams will help you understand what's on your mind and may help you discover what's causing your nightmares.

I Don't Want to Talk About IT!

Wetting the bed can be embarrassing. And because IT's something most boys don't talk about, IT can make you feel like you're the only boy in the world who does IT. Well, you're not the only one! There are millions of boys of all ages (even teenagers) who wet the bed every single night.

No one wets the bed on purpose. It's something you can't stop doing—at least for now. Most boys that wet the bed are heavy sleepers who just don't wake up in time to make it to the bathroom to pee. Don't be discouraged if you have this problem. It's very likely you'll grow out of IT very soon.

To help things along, don't drink anything after dinner and go to the bathroom just before bedtime. If you're having a hard time with bedwetting, ask your parents to take you to see your family doctor. There are a number of approaches you can try to cure bedwetting, including bladder exercises and alarms that wake you if you pee in the middle of the night. There are also medicines that can help. But remember that while medicines treat the problem they don't cure IT. Medicines work best when they're combined with exercises or an alarm.

BAD STUFF

Tobacco, alcohol, and drugs are really bad for your still-growing body. They can damage your brain, heart, and most of your other organs, too. Inhalants, like aerosol sprays, can kill you in a matter of minutes by cutting off oxygen to your brain. Cocaine, an illegal drug, can cause a boy your age to have a heart attack. And prescription drugs, like those in your parent's medicine cabinet, can kill you. Never take a prescription drug that isn't prescribed just for you by a doctor.

You may someday find yourself in a situation where a friend is putting pressure on you to smoke, drink alcohol, or take drugs. The offer can be tempting, especially if it seems like everybody's doing it. But remember that most kids don't smoke, drink, or do drugs. And don't believe it if someone says you're immature for not trying it. The fact is it takes more courage to stand up for what you believe in, and it's smart to take care of yourself by saying NO!

When someone offers you a cigarette, beer, or drugs, here are some ways to say NO!

1. No, thanks, I have better things to do!
2. Don't push me! My answer is NO!
3. It's not my thing!
4. I don't feel like it!
5. Leave me alone!
6. Are you talking to me? Forget it!

Other things you can do:

1. Walk away.

2. Don't hang out with kids that put pressure on you to use tobacco, alcohol, or illegal drugs.

3. Talk to your parents about what's going on.

4. Talk to your coach, teacher, counselor, or principal about tobacco, alcohol, and illegal drug use in your school.

5. Don't let TV, magazines, or online advertisements trick you into thinking alcohol or tobacco is OK for you.

6. Find out the facts about tobacco, alcohol, and illegal drugs and the good reasons not to use them.

If you want to learn more about tobacco, have your parents help you visit www.tobaccofreekids.org (The Campaign for Tobacco-Free Kids). For more on alcohol, check out Leadership To Keep Children Alcohol Free at www.alcoholfreechildren.org. And if you want to know more about illegal drugs, visit the National Institute on Drug Abuse at www.nida.nih.gov.

PERSONAL NOTES

NOTES

NOTES

NOTES

NOTES